KING
of the
BENCH

COMEBACK KID

KING
of the
BENCH

COMEBACK KID

STEVE MOORE

HARPER
An Imprint of HarperCollinsPublishers

ISBN 978-0-06-220336-6

Typography by Katie Klimowicz
18 19 20 21 22   CG/LSCH   10 9 8 7 6 5 4 3 2 1
❖
First Edition

To Melaine . . . A thousand years.

PROLOGUE

My name is Steve, and I am a bench-warmer.

I'm a seventh grader at Spiro T. Agnew Middle School—Home of the Mighty Plumbers. That's the nickname for our sports teams, and I'm not even making that up.

A long time ago, way back in the ancient 1970s, a genius school official thought the image of a plumber in overalls holding a pipe wrench would strike fear in the hearts of Spiro's opponents.

Derp!

If you've read any of my other books—*No Fear!* or *Control Freak* or *Kicking & Screaming*—then you already know that I love sports, but I rarely get to play.

(And if you haven't read any of the other books, then I am really embarrassed for you.)

Don't feel all sorry for me or anything, but the score's got to be about a hundred to zip before a coach even thinks about putting me in a game.

Either that, or a string of freak injuries to starters has to leave a coach no choice but to put me in. Like when a soccer player named Thunderfoot shredded the hands of the starting goalie and I was the only substitute available.

In this book, I'm going to tell you about a basketball season when I alone was responsible for my rear end being planted on the pine, which is another way of saying I sat on the bench. But first, let me ask you a question:

Have you ever been given a crummy chore and you did too good of a job at it?

Like scooping dog poop or digging a putrid wad of hair out of a clogged shower drain or crawling into an attic to dispose of rat carcasses?

It's practically a rule that if you do too good of a job with a crummy chore, you will be stuck doing that crummy chore for the rest of your life. And there will be no one to blame but yourself.

That's what happened to me during the Mighty Plumbers basketball season. I got stuck sitting on the pine because I did way too good of a job as—

Derp!

I almost blew it.

I can't reveal any more details right now because—big, drooly *duh*—it's pretty much a strict rule when writing a book that you don't just blurt out all the juicy plot stuff in the first few pages.

So I'll tell you more later, like when I get in the mood or when you can't stand the suspense for even a half second longer. Whichever comes first.

All you need to know for now is that I'm not a drooling dweeb, okay? Even though I'm a benchwarmer, I do have some skills.

For example, I have excellent leaping ability.

That would be a huge advantage if I was

to rob a batter of a home run by jumping up and catching the ball just before it sails over the right-field fence.

Or if I was running with the football and I leaped over a linebacker and landed in the end zone for a touchdown.

Or if I was swimming in the Amazon River and someone shouted, "Piranha!"

So don't feel sorry for me. I'm not all bitter and gloomy just because I sit on the bench. Besides, I'm probably better at it than anyone else my age in the entire city—maybe even the entire world.

End of the pine or middle of the pine. Doesn't matter

I'm King of the Bench!

No brag. It's just a fact.

CHAPTER

Silence, random kid!

I'm not in the mood to blurt out juicy plot stuff yet, so you'll just have to wait.

And wait.

And wait.

And . . .

Ha! Just goofing.

I'm in the mood now.

In the first game of the Spiro T. Agnew basketball season, I literally stumbled upon a ritual that could change the momentum of a basketball game and result in an amazing comeback victory. And I'm not even exaggerating.

But before I can tell you about the first game of the season, I have to back up a minute. Sorry. I guess you'll have to wait a little bit longer after all.

Twenty-three students had tried out for the Spiro team, but Coach Earwax had chosen only eight to be Mighty Plumbers—including my three best friends and me.

WE RULE!

SPIRO

THE STOOL!!

BECKY   JOEY   CARLOS   ME

Quick Time-Out about My Friends

Becky O'Callahan is a hotshot athlete, but she doesn't have that hotshot attitude my dad calls "entitlement." That's when someone expects to get a free ticket to a movie or the best seat on the team bus or a passing grade in math simply because they are a hotshot athlete.

(My dad knows all about hotshot athletes because he was one before the ligaments in both of his knees snapped like rubber bands, ruining his chance to earn billions of dollars playing professional sports.)

Becky is by far the best athlete at Spiro. Baseball, football, soccer, basketball, track, hockey, golf. Doesn't matter. She's the best.

And she has Nature's Near-Perfect Smile.

My other two friends and I are not gifted athletes. Not even close. But we love everything about sports, except when Coach makes us do a million push-ups or run wind sprints until our lungs practically explode.

Even sitting on the bench for hours at a time can be fun if you love being around sports. Joey, Carlos, and I kill time by cracking jokes or pulling pranks or seeing who can hold their breath the longest without blacking out and keeling over onto the floor.

Joey is a small guy, and I'm talking teensy, but he can run faster than any other middle school student in our entire city. Maybe even the entire world. It's a survival skill found in all tiny creatures. Joey is like a flea. If you blink, he's gone.

He's also a psychic, and I'm not even making that up. Joey can predict stuff like if a basketball player is going to dribble to the left or the right or pass the ball to a teammate cutting to the hoop.

Carlos is the opposite of Joey. Carlos is slow and sort of big-boned. And he's a grouch. He's a good guy, but Carlos never stops complaining. He's the official Mighty Plumbers team grouch.

Carlos does have one amazing talent. He can burp and speak at the same time. I'm talking entire paragraphs in a single belch!

Carlos's belches are morale builders. Like if our team is getting creamed, he burp-speaks so loud the sound waves can shatter glass.

KISH!!

HELLO?...CAN YOU HEAR ME??

• • •

With so many students trying out for the basketball team, it was miraculous that Joey, Carlos, and I made the cut. But Coach Earwax actually *begged* Becky to play on the team, which is a humiliating thing for any coach to do.

Coach didn't even have to beg, though, because Becky loves basketball and was looking forward to the season.

Meanwhile, Coach Earwax didn't even know that Joey, Carlos, and I wanted to try out, because we forgot to put our names on the sign-up sheet beforehand.

Coach has a hearing problem due to a serious blockage.

He frequently digs huge chunks of wax out of his ears with his car key, then rolls them up and sticks the wads under the bench like spent chewing gum. If Coach didn't dig the wax out of his ears, it would back way up into his brain and block his ability to make brilliant coaching decisions.

After Coach finally heard our pathetic begging, he let Joey, Carlos, and I try out. Joey was quick as a flea, Carlos used his big-boned body to play good defense, and my leaping ability helped me block a few shots.

And just like in every other sport, we barely made the cut for Spiro's basketball team.

But there was one guy who made the starting lineup without even showing up for tryouts.

CHAPTER 2

Jimmy Jimerino is Spiro's BJOC—Big Jock on Campus in every sport. Jimmy was in the grip of that whole "entitlement" thing that my dad told me about.

Jimmy skipped tryouts because he believed that he was the best basketball player at Spiro T. Agnew Middle School.

I think Coach Earwax had some sort of a brain wreck, because he actually went along with Jimmy's hotshot entitlement.

Jimmy strolled into the Spiro gym on the

first day of practice like God's gift to basketball. He was fifteen minutes late. He was
chewing gum. And he was talking on his cell
phone.

Meanwhile, the rest of us were doing the
cruelest, most lung-exploding conditioning
drill ever invented by a basketball coach.

Here's a brief description:

Sprint from baseline to top of key, back
to baseline, then to half-court line, back to
baseline, then to top of key on other end of
court, then back to baseline, then to baseline
on other end of court, then back to the starting baseline.

(Just describing the drill makes my lungs
burn.)

The drill was made even more difficult because the Spiro gymnasium is a dump.

Quick Time-Out about the Spiro Gym

First of all, the Spiro gym is really old.

Historians say the gym was built along with the rest of the school back in the ancient 1970s, which makes it even older than my mom and dad.

The floors, ceilings, walls, bleachers, and locker rooms are coated in many layers of sweat that gushed out of the pores of grimy middle schoolers during dodgeball, basketball, volleyball, and wrestling. Especially wrestling.

In case you don't already know, middle-schooler sweat has a huge corrosive effect on wood, paint, plaster, cement, and other building materials. It's way worse than adult sweat, which mostly just stinks.

The ceiling tiles in the gym are warped like bacon and tilted as if they might fall at any second. Lights flicker or shut off for no apparent reason. The floors are creaky. And the locker room plumbing is corroded and clogged with all kinds of gnarly bodily stuff that I don't even want to talk about.

The gym is also home to all kinds of vermin such as cockroaches, ants, flies, and rats.

The so-called "climate-control system" is the worst problem in the Spiro gym. It never works correctly. Ever.

If it's cold outside, the system freaks out and pumps COLD air inside. If it's hot outside, the system blows a gasket and pumps HOT air inside.

Mr. Joseph, Spiro's groundskeeper and building maintenance manager, works hard to fight the middle-school sweat corrosion and to keep the plumbing and electrical systems from total failure. But the entire gymnasium needs to be torn down and rebuilt.

• • •

On the first day of basketball practice, the temperature outside was hot. So the climate-control system, of course, blasted hot air into the Spiro gym while we were doing the conditioning drill that practically exploded our lungs.

When Jimmy arrived at practice, Coach Earwax pulled him aside.

Everyone thought Jimmy would have to sprint up and down the court until his lungs practically exploded in order to make up for not bothering to try out and for being fifteen minutes late to the first practice and for chewing gum and talking on his cell phone.

But that didn't happen.

Coach Earwax told Jimmy to do a few wimpy stretching exercises that any two-year-old could do without even soiling his diapers.

And that was it. That was Jimmy's consequence.

Jimmy finished stretching in about ten seconds, then Coach blew his whistle and told us to break off into the positions we wanted to play: point guard, shooting guard, center, power forward, small forward.

Jimmy claimed the point guard position, of course, because it's like playing quarterback in football or center midfielder in soccer or pitcher in baseball.

Joey got in line behind Jimmy. He had no choice. If you're a tiny guy who wants to play basketball, then it's a strict rule that you play point guard.

Stephanie Jennison chose the shooting guard position even though she can dribble and pass and shoot a basketball better than Jimmy. (But he'd never admit it.)

Carlos chose the center position. He wasn't the tallest player on the team, but a big-boned body comes in handy when you're trying to shove your way under the hoop for a rebound or a dunk. Although in Carlos's case, a dunk was unlikely.

EIGHT-INCH VERTICAL LEAP

Unfortunately for Carlos, Skinny Dennis was locked in as the starting center because he had just gone through a freaky growth spurt.

He wasn't just taller than Carlos. Skinny was taller than Coach Earwax!

He didn't gain much weight with the extra height, though. Skinny just sort of got all stretched out like string cheese. He finally lived up to his name! (Which isn't a nickname, by the way.)

Becky O'Callahan chose small forward. That's a position where you not only need to be good at scoring, but also rebounding and blocking shots. Becky can do all three.

I chose power forward even though there is nothing powerful about me. I'm average height. Average weight. And my muscles are still waiting to receive that Magic Signal from my brain.

I wanted to play power forward because I love grabbing rebounds. Like I said, I might be a benchwarmer, but I have excellent leaping ability. And if you want to grab rebounds, it's a strict rule that you have to be able to jump.

Rebounding isn't the most glamorous skill in basketball, but it's important. If no one grabbed rebounds, the basketball would ricochet off the backboard and bounce around the gym until a random kid in the bleachers picked it up and took the ball home as a souvenir.

Dewey Taylor was my competition for starting power forward. Dewey is taller than me. A few of his muscles had received that Magic Signal from his brain to buff out. We're both pretty good at scoring, but Dewey can't jump as high as me.

For the first time in my extraordinarily average athletic career, I thought there was a chance I could be a starter.

In the first practice, we mostly worked on conditioning drills that were designed to whip our weak and useless bodies into fine-tuned athletic machines.

SIT-UPS

PUSH-UPS

LEG LIFTS

YOGA

NOT REALLY

We all were gulping for oxygen by the end of practice. Sweat was gushing out of our skin, which wasn't necessarily a bad thing. In case you don't already know, gushing sweat is a Badge of Honor in basketball. Unless it gets too out of control.

We staggered toward the locker room. The climate-control system blasted hot air. My mouth was dry, and I tried to hack up some spit so that my tongue wouldn't crumble into mummy dust. But all I got was a dirty taste like when you suck on a rock. (Not that I've ever done that.)

While I was trying to hack up spit, I saw a scraggly gym rat beat cheeks across the basketball court and dart under the bleachers behind our team bench.

I didn't think much about it at the time because, like I said, the Spiro gym is a dump and home to all kinds of gnarly vermin.

But the rat would turn out to play an important role in my discovery of the ritual that could create a rally, change the momentum of a basketball game, and result in an amazing comeback victory.

CHAPTER

I would love to tell you that Joey, Carlos, and I broke into the Mighty Plumbers' starting lineup, but that would be a gigantic whopper. We were the team's three subs—or "scrubs," as Jimmy Jimerino called us.

Once again, my friends and I were the three Benchkateers!

Our rear ends were glued to the bench when we opened the season at home against the Werewolves of Chaney Middle School.

Chaney is one of the meanest schools in the entire world, and I'm not even exaggerating. The Werewolves had a reputation for poor sportsmanship. Just making direct eye contact with one of their players could provoke a shoving match that escalated into a bench-clearing brawl.

The Spiro starters were Jimmy, Becky, Skinny, Stephanie, and Dewey. Skinny lined up for the tip-off against Chaney's biggest player, a man-kid named Beast.

Beast was middle-school age, but he looked like he was somewhere between twenty-seven and thirty-one years old. He was six feet tall and had beefy arms that were covered in hair all the way up to his shoulders. (And don't even ask me about his armpits.)

Skinny Dennis and Beast were the same height, but Beast outweighed Skinny by probably a hundred pounds. It looked like the

Werewolves' center could grab our center in one hand and snap him like a puny twig.

But it turned out that Beast's brawn and masses of body hair weighed him down.

When the ref tossed up the basketball, Skinny jumped two feet higher than Beast and tipped the ball to Jimmy Jimerino.

Jimmy dribbled through the weak and useless Werewolves, weaving like a soccer midfielder, and scored an easy layup.

The entire Spiro crowd was on its feet cheering. Everyone except two people.

The first was Mother T, our school principal. Mother T is tiny and frail and never shows emotion.

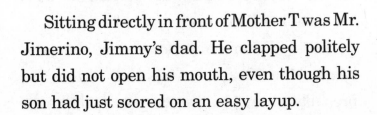

Sitting directly in front of Mother T was Mr. Jimerino, Jimmy's dad. He clapped politely but did not open his mouth, even though his son had just scored on an easy layup.

Why? Because Jimmy's dad was on "disciplinary probation."

Mr. Jimerino had been a loudmouth during the baseball and football seasons. He'd yelled at the umpires and the refs and even his own son if Jimmy did something wrong.

But during the soccer season, in the championship match of a major tournament, Mr. Jimerino totally blew a head gasket. The ref gave him a red card and kicked him off the sidelines—the first time in the history of the league that a parent got ejected!

After that embarrassing incident, Mother T banned Mr. Jimerino from all Spiro T. Agnew athletic events unless he agreed to one condition: He had to sit directly in front of Mother T.

On the inbounds pass after Jimmy's easy layup, Becky stepped in front of a Chaney player and stole the ball. She took two quick steps to the hoop and scored.

Then Dewey Taylor blocked a Chaney shot and Stephanie Jennison scooped up the ball, dribbled the length of the court, and dunked—*dunked!*

We were ahead, six to zip, and it wasn't even ten seconds into the game.

The Mighty Plumbers had seized the "Big Mo"—the game momentum—a mysterious phenomenon that suddenly makes everything go your way.

Meanwhile, back on the pine, my friends and I settled into the internationally recognized Rules of Behavior for basketball benchwarmers:

We cheered. We jumped up and pumped our fists in the air every time our team scored or blocked a shot or stole the ball. And when the other team scored or stole the ball, we slouched with our arms folded across our chests and looked all sullen and bitter.

In between all of our official bench behavior, Joey, Carlos, and I occupied ourselves with other *unofficial* bench stuff.

We tied and retied our shoelaces, which is sort of an obsessive thing that Joey started. We glanced back over our shoulders to check out the fans in the bleachers. And we swigged Gatorade, even though we were sitting on our rear ends and not doing anything that would deplete even one drop of our essential bodily fluids.

I was retying my shoelaces for at least the fourth time when I spotted the gym rat.

Yeah, the same rat I saw at the end of our first practice. Or maybe it was a different one. I don't know. Rats all look alike.

Anyway, the gnarly rodent crawled out from under the bleachers and darted under the far end of our bench, where Ricky Schnauzer, the team manager, had neatly stored the towels, water bottles, and tasty protein bars that Spiro players needed to keep their bodies in prime athletic condition.

I bent over, looked under the bench, and saw the rat grab one of the protein bars in its mouth. Then it dashed back under the bleachers.

Okay, not only are those protein bars tasty, but they are expensive! The Spiro T. Agnew athletic department isn't exactly loaded with cash, so that rat basically had committed a felony.

I told Joey and Carlos about the gym rat. Carlos was really peeved when he found out there was one less protein bar for him to scarf. Joey just shrugged because he knew it was going to happen five minutes before the rat stole the protein bar.

(Joey is really soft-spoken, so his important predictions are hard to hear.)

After the gym-rat robbery, all three of us kept our eyes on the pricey protein bars in case the rodent returned to the buffet for a second helping.

Meanwhile, in the second half, the game took a frightening turn.

Remember when I mentioned the Big Mo? I hope so, because it was only a few pages back, so it would be really annoying if you already forgot.

Well, the Mighty Plumbers had momentum for the first half of the game. But the Werewolves started the second half with a major rally.

CHAPTER 4

Our halftime lead of 30–2 was quickly shrinking.

The Werewolves had a steal, a layup, another steal, another layup, and another steal. Then Beast somehow got his brawn and masses of body hair high enough off the ground to slam down a gruesome dunk that rattled the walls of the gymnasium.

I think the vibration even set off a car alarm out in the parking lot, but that might have been a coincidence.

The Werewolves had seized the Big Mo.

Ordinarily, in that situation, Carlos would have ripped one of his famous belches that can boost the morale of his struggling teammates.

Carlos has enough gas bottled up in his gut to burp the weird names of disgusting vegetables.

But he couldn't tap into his amazing gift that night in the gym.

Our school principal had learned about Carlos's amazing ability, and she'd banned him from belching during indoor school functions. Mother T apparently was worried that the sonic waves from his epic burps might cause the school's ancient 1970s structures to collapse.

When it became obvious that Spiro had lost the Big Mo, Coach Earwax called a time-out to design a strategy that would stop the Werewolves' rally.

On the sideline, he knelt down on one knee with his white board and did that basketball-coach thing where he scribbled diagrams that only he could understand.

At the end of the time-out, Coach Earwax motioned for Carlos and me to go in the game at center and power forward. Substituting players is a common tactic that coaches use to change the momentum of a game.

But Carlos and I had zero effect on the Big Mo.

Every time Carlos tried to stop Beast from scoring, the Chaney center would raise the ball overhead and smoosh his hairy arm-pits into Carlos's face. That disgusting tactic triggered Carlos's "gag reflex." You know. That thing where you retch and almost blow chunks, but all that comes out are dry heaves that sound like a barnyard animal.

While Carlos retched and bleated like a goat, Beast dribbled around him and scored.

When I replaced Dewey Taylor as power forward, I was determined to grab rebounds on both ends of the court.

A key part of my strategy was to put on my "game face" to intimidate my opponent and establish a psychological edge. A game face is pretty much standard in any sport.

It's like when a peacock fans out his rainbow tail feathers and puffs out his chest to strike terror into weak and useless predators.

Or maybe that's a peacock mating ritual. I'm not sure.

Anyway, I have my own assortment of game faces that I use in pretty much every sport.

BASEBALL   FOOTBALL   SOCCER

And here's the basketball game face I used against the Werewolves.

I have no idea why, but it didn't work.

The Werewolves' power forward and I were the same height and weight, but he had a slight advantage. His game face was WAY more intimidating than mine.

And I'm not even exaggerating!

Every time I tried to leap up for a rebound, he would growl and gnash his teeth. Then I would lose concentration and let the basketball slip out of my grip.

I did manage to do one thing right. After

one of the Werewolves' baskets, I inbounded the ball to Jimmy without accidentally tossing it to an opponent.

But that was it. No points. No steals. No assists. No rebounds.

At the next change of possession, Coach Earwax took me out and Dewey went back in at power forward.

The Werewolves still had the Big Mo, and we were getting mauled, 80–50.

I planted my rear end back down on the bench and wiped the sweat off my face with a clean and fragrant towel that team manager Ricky Schnauzer handed me as soon as I walked off the court.

Carlos was also yanked and put back on the bench, but he was relieved to be far, far away from Beast's hairy armpits.

Meanwhile, Joey remained on the bench because Jimmy Jimerino was still at point guard and in control of the Mighty Plumbers' offense.

Soft-spoken Joey made another one of his stupefying psychic predictions.

Sure enough, about ten seconds later, I spotted the felonious rat.

It dashed out of the bleachers and disappeared under the far end of the bench, where Ricky had stored our clean and fragrant towels, water bottles, and tasty protein bars.

I didn't need to duck my head under the bench to see what the rat was up to.

I jumped up. The gym rat poked its head out from under the bench. It had a protein bar in its mouth. I wasn't going to let it steal another one.

There was no time to hesitate, because rodents are almost as quick as Joey. The rat darted for its hideout under the bleachers, and I dove to save the protein bar.

I slid about ten feet on my belly, like a baseball player diving headfirst to snag a line drive. It was an excellent slide. (No brag. It's just a fact.) But I missed the protein bar by a fraction of an inch, and the rat escaped with its plunder.

My excellent belly slide did not go unnoticed. I turned my head toward the bleachers. The spectators were all staring at me. Even Joey and Carlos and Coach Earwax were looking at me.

Everyone was silent for about two seconds, then burst into cheers!

I stood up and sort of gave a little bow.

No one had seen the rat steal the protein bar, so they had no idea why I had slid on my belly. I guess they thought I was pulling some kind of goofy stunt, like when the Mighty Plumbers mascot stumbles all around the court at halftime and acts like a fool.

But right after I took my bow, something amazing happened.

Chaney's beastly center muscled his way in front of the basket and turned to shoot. But Skinny stood his ground against Beast's brawn and his hairy, stanky armpits.

He blocked his shot!

Becky grabbed the rebound and passed it to Dewey. Dewey dribbled a few steps and passed the ball to Stephanie. Then Stephanie flipped it to Jimmy, who scored on an easy layup.

Spiro had reclaimed the Big Mo.

The Mighty Plumbers stopped the Werewolves on the next ten possessions. And Jimmy went on a shooting frenzy, scoring every time he got his hands on the ball.

He scored twenty unanswered points in the final minutes, and Spiro defeated the Werewolves, 89–88.

It was the biggest comeback in the history of Spiro T. Agnew Middle School!

After the game, there were the usual fist bumps and high fives. Spiro boosters ran down out of the bleachers and onto the court. But they didn't just swarm the Mighty Plumbers' starting five.

They all believed that my excellent slide had sparked a rally that changed the momentum of the game. Derp!

CHAPTER 5

The next day was Sunday, so Joey, Carlos, Becky, and I met up and walked to Goodfellow Stadium to watch an NBA game. The stadium is right smack in the middle of our neighborhood.

When we're not at school or home in bed, we practically live at Goodfellow Stadium. It's got a rickety domed roof that slides open and closed, so it can host pretty much any kind of sport in any kind of weather.

Since it was basketball season and

winter was closing in, the domed roof was closed. That meant two things for the twenty thousand spectators crammed inside the stadium:

First, they were relatively safe if a freak blizzard suddenly struck during the game. The dome would offer some protection against seventy-mile-per-hour winds, twenty-foot snowdrifts, and deadly hypothermia.

And second, the stadium air would be moldy and smelly because twenty thousand spectators with bad breath and body odor were crammed inside.

But my friends and I weren't worried about snowdrifts or hypothermia. And we had pretty much learned to ignore the moldy stank of twenty thousand bodies.

We were there to watch the Goodfellow Goons slaughter the weak and useless Los Angeles Lakers, a former hotshot team that had fallen on hard times.

On the way to Goodfellow, Becky asked me about "that thing" I did during the Chaney game.

I started to tell her the story of the gym rat and the tasty protein bar and how I tried to stop a felony in progress. But she interrupted me halfway through.

"Whatever you did, keep doing it!"

My friends and I entered Goodfellow Stadium without paying for a ticket. Not because we were Mighty Plumbers basketball players and expected free tickets. We earned our way in.

Before every game, the concession workers unload truckloads of supplies to feed the twenty thousand spectators who stink up the air inside Goodfellow Stadium.

My friends and I help them carry in the boxes in exchange for a free game pass and a treat of our choice.

That night, when we were done hauling boxes, Joey selected his usual treat—a churro, which is a deep-fried pastry smothered in sugar. Carlos went for his favorite, a family-size bag of salted peanuts. He likes to suck all the salt off and then eat the peanuts, shell and all.

Becky and I chose an Eskimo Pie, as usual—our favorite stadium treat in the entire universe. Vanilla ice cream covered in chocolate. It's nature's near-perfect food.

By the way, Becky and I are not "a thing," if you know what I mean. So don't even think that. We're just good friends who both happen to like Eskimo Pies, okay?

Anyway, after getting our snacks, we all walked up to our seats at the very top level of Goodfellow Stadium, where the lice-infested pigeons roost.

Some people refer to those seats as the "nosebleed section" because it's so high up that blood vessels in nasal passages can burst open and spew blood all over the bleachers.

(I don't know if that's true or not. It might be one of those myths that spectators in the lower seats believe so they feel better about paying a lot more money for their seats.)

The game had already begun by the time Joey, Carlos, Becky, and I made our climb into the polluted upper atmosphere of Good-fellow Stadium.

Down on the court, the Goons were slaughtering the Lakers. This was something new.

In past seasons, the Goons were a "door-mat" team. They hardly ever won.

My friends and I supported them, though. Even if they got creamed by a hundred to zip. They were our hometown team. And the players were friendly and generous. They would give you the socks right off their feet.

But this year, in the off-season, the Goons had forked over about a billion dollars in hard-earned cash for a hotshot player who'd almost single-handedly turned the team from a doormat into a contender.

His name was Vido Artukovich.

Quick Time-Out about Vido

Vido Artukovich is seven feet tall, which is the perfect height to play center, but Vido is a point guard because he is quick and handles the basketball like a magician. He is by far the best player in the league. Maybe even the best player in NBA history, although my dad disagrees.

Dad believes that Kobe Bryant was the greatest player in the entire universe. But he can't prove it because Kobe played way back in ancient times, so he's really old and rickety now.

There's no way Kobe could go one-on-one

against Vido Artukovich to settle the argument because Kobe probably wouldn't even be able to bend over and tie his shoelaces.

(Dad tries to convince me by "comparing career statistics," but my brain shuts down when confronted with any kind of math.)

Vido is the star of the Goons, but he has a severe case of hotshot entitlement. He is a ball hog. In a single game, he could get a hundred points and a hundred rebounds and a hundred steals and a hundred blocked shots and a grand total of zero assists.

And he is a show-off. Every time he scores, Vido pounds his chest like King Kong.

He isn't friendly and generous like his Goons teammates. At the end of one Good-fellow game, my friends and I beat cheeks down to the floor and gave high fives to the players as they were walking to the locker room.

All of the players except Vido. He walked right past and left us hanging.

You can probably tell that Vido Artukovich

doesn't exactly fry my burger.

If Vido was to take off his sweaty socks and offer them to me (not that it would ever happen), I would walk away and leave him hanging.

• • •

My friends and I settled in to watch Vido (er, the Goons) cream the weak and useless Lakers.

Joey did one of his psychic things. I thought he said "Chill." Becky heard "Dill." And Carlos didn't hear anything because he was preoccupied.

STEP 1 : SUCK SALT OFF SHELL.
STEP 2 : CHEW PEANUT.
STEP 3 : SWALLOW PEANUT, SHELL AND ALL.

About thirty seconds later, our good friend Bill—Billionaire Bill—strolled toward us. He was pointing an air horn up at the rafters.

Bill was on patrol, but he took a break and sat down with us.

Bill is a gonzo sports fan who lives inside Goodfellow Stadium in a tiny apartment under the bleachers. In exchange for free rent, he works as the official "pigeon-control officer."

He patrols the upper deck and blasts an air horn to scare lice-infested pigeons out of the rafters so that spectators down below don't have to worry about what might drop from up above. If you know what I mean.

Bill told us he once was a very wealthy and respected man. I think he was either a fighter pilot or a Hall of Fame basketball coach. Maybe a balloon salesman. I forget.

Anyway, Bill chucked the good life, and now he hangs out in Goodfellow Stadium and scares the poop out of lice-infested pigeons.

Bill took a seat and looked down on the court where the Lakers were getting smeared by Vido Artukovich. Then he gave us another one of his valuable nuggets of wisdom.

Whoa.

That was deep.

But we had no idea what he was talking about. Not even Becky!

Bill could tell we were struggling, so he explained that he got the nugget of wisdom from a guy named John Wooden, who coached a college basketball team way back before the World Wide Web was invented.

Bill was about to tell us the name of the college where Wooden coached, but a couple of lice-infested pigeons flew onto the rafters up above and threatened us. If you know what I mean.

Bill ran off in pursuit of the pigeons. It was his job.

He ditched my friends and me because his tiny apartment under the bleachers wasn't just handed to him. He had to earn it.

That's why, next to my mom and dad, Billionaire Bill is pretty much my favorite adult role model in the entire universe.

My friends and I watched the rest of the Goons' game. It wasn't a pretty sight.

At one point, Vido (er, Goodfellow) was ahead by thirty points. Then the Big Mo changed directions. The Lakers rallied and battled back, and Goodfellow ended up losing to Los Angeles, 101–100.

Every one of the Lakers players had contributed in the win. Meanwhile, Vido had scored ninety-nine of the Goons' one hundred points. But they still lost.

Billionaire Bill's valuable nugget of advice started to make sense.

"The main ingredient in stardom is the rest of the team."

CHAPTER 6

At school on Monday, Jimmy Jimerino claimed credit for the basketball team's comeback win over the Chaney Werewolves.

He strolled into the cafeteria at lunch like one of those superheroes in the movies who just single-handedly defeated a madman and his clone army when they tried to destroy the world.

My friends and I sat in our usual spot at the C Central table. It's right along Jimmy's path to the Jock Table, where he rules over a posse of slobbering kiss-ups.

As Jimmy walked toward our table, he looked at Becky O'Callahan. (He and Becky once were "a thing," but she had figured out pretty quickly that Jimmy didn't exactly fry her burger.)

Becky pretended to drop her napkin on the floor, and she ducked under the table to avoid eye contact with Jimmy.

Then Jimmy looked right at me.

I had just taken a huge bite out of that day's Mighty Plumbers Special—"the Tyrannosaurus Mex." It was a gigantic taco with tons of meat, beans, lettuce, tomatoes, imitation cheese product, and hot sauce. (It was one of the few cafeteria meals that actually fried my burger, so to speak.)

THE TYRANNOSAURUS MEX

ABOUT THE SIZE OF A → FOOTBALL

Melted imitation cheese product and hot sauce oozed out of both corners of my mouth and dribbled onto my T-shirt. I was defenseless.

Jimmy stopped and pointed at me.

"Hey, there he is—Mr. Belly Slider!"

His kiss-up posse laughed their rear ends off.

Then Jimmy and his crew strolled off to plant their rear ends on benches at the Jock Table.

Becky resurfaced from her fake napkin rescue mission. Joey resumed taking tiny bites out of the peanut-butter-and-anchovy sandwich that his mom had packed. And Carlos never even paused his frontal assault on his three—*three*—Tyrannosaurus Mex tacos.

CHAPTER 7

Later that day, Jimmy strolled into math class fifteen minutes late. He was chewing gum, which is a minor violation of school rules. And he was talking on his cell phone, which is strictly forbidden during class.

Then he pointed at me and winked.

"Mr. Belly Slider!"

Mr. Spleen, the math teacher, was in the middle of scrawling alien symbols on the whiteboard.

I kept waiting for Jimmy to be reprimanded for being fifteen minutes late, or, at the very least, for chewing gum. But that didn't happen.

Jimmy sat in his seat directly in front of me and slouched down so that Mr. Spleen could not see that he had switched his phone conversation to text messaging.

He did stop chewing gum, but only because he had chewed the flavor down to zero. Jimmy pulled the worthless gum wad out of his mouth and stuck it under his chair.

The entire class sort of just shrugged off the incident because Jimmy is a hotshot athlete.

But one student decided to speak up.

Jessica Whitehead, the school genius, raised her hand.

I GET STRAIGHT As, SO CAN I ARRIVE LATE FOR CLASS AND TALK ON MY CELL PHONE AND CHEW GUM?

Jessica is very smart, but she sometimes can act like an entitled athlete.

Mr. Spleen thought about Jessica's question for about $15 - 13 = 2$ seconds. Then he just chuckled, turned his back, and scrawled more alien symbols on the whiteboard.

Jessica was $15 - 15 = 0$ happy about Mr. Spleen's answer.

CHAPTER

When I got home after school, I barricaded myself in my room. Well, it wasn't a barricade. The door doesn't even have a lock. I just shut it firmly.

It wasn't like I was blocking out the world and acting all mopey and depressed because of Jimmy's Mr. Belly Slider slam. I was just trying to keep one of my pets from escaping my bedroom and scaring my mom right out of her skull.

Fido is the best pet in the entire universe, and I'm not even exaggerating. He's a boa constrictor, which is a snake that can grow to ten feet. That's big enough to swallow a small poodle.

YAP! YAP! YAP!

Fido's not that big. Yet. For now he can only swallow a mouse or maybe a rat.

I keep my bedroom door closed because Fido often escapes from his terrarium. If I leave my door open, he roams our house searching for me because we're bonded and he's got "separation anxiety." That's a psychological disorder common in boa constrictors and most first graders.

I have two other pets inside my bedroom: A bug-eyed goldfish named Zoner who has narcolepsy, which causes her to fall asleep unexpectedly, and Frenchy, a poodle who is just about the right size for a ten-foot boa constrictor to swallow.

Zoner is one of those "low-maintenance pets." She just needs to be fed and, when she suddenly falls asleep and turns belly up, I just need to make sure no one thinks she's kacked.

But Frenchy is high-maintenance and totally demented. He lives under my bed and never comes out except to "do his business" in the backyard. (And then I have to clean it up.)

Frenchy demands that his food and water be delivered to him under the bed. Why? I don't know. You'd have to ask Frenchy, but all you'd get in response would be growling and snapping teeth.

Frenchy is the most entitled dog in the entire universe, and I'm not even exaggerating. He's worse than entitled hotshot athletes, because I'm pretty sure they don't "do their business" in the backyard and then make someone else clean it up.

That afternoon, I finished my homework in about two minutes. It helped that the only assignment I had was a study sheet for a test in history. Mr. Chisholm, the history teacher, always makes the study sheets an exact replica of the test, so all I had to do was memorize the answers.

I had a lot of time before dinner, so I decided to take my basketball outside and practice rebounding. I figured if I worked hard and got really good at leaping up and grabbing rebounds then Coach Earwax would have no other choice than to put me in the game.

But first, I had to find my basketball.

I normally keep it in my closet underneath the pile of rancid athletic socks that drives my mom right out of her skull. But it wasn't there. I looked everywhere in my room with no luck.

Then I got down on my hands and knees and looked under my bed.

Frenchy immediately growled and snorted. He somehow had dug the basketball out from underneath my rancid sock pile without kacking from the toxic fumes. Then he'd pushed it into his demented poodle cave beneath my bed.

Frenchy wasn't going to give up the basketball without a fight. What a ball hog!

I tried to reach under and grab the basketball, but Frenchy growled even louder and snapped his teeth. He's never actually bitten anyone, but I wasn't going to take a chance, because a wounded hand would hurt my ability to rebound.

So I went and got a broom and used the handle to rescue my basketball from the mad poodle. I knocked it out from under my bed, but Frenchy pretty much shredded the broom handle with his canine teeth.

CHAPTER 9

My house has a large backyard with a pond where my pet duck, Cleo, sticks her head underwater all day and scarfs up mysterious edible scum off the bottom. Cleo is very intelligent. She has the IQ of a ninth grader, and I'm not even exaggerating.

Oh, and Cleo thinks she's a dog.

Anyway, I also have a portable basketball hoop in my backyard. It's backed up against the fence between my house and our neighbor's. Mrs. Smoot is a recluse, which means she never leaves her house—not to plant flowers in her front yard or to vote in local elections or to work out at a gym.

Never.

No one in the neighborhood even knows what she looks like. But I do know that Mrs. Smoot has about ten million cats, by my estimate. She is a pet hoarder.

I went out into my backyard with my basketball and stood in front of the portable hoop.

There is only one way I know to practice rebounding by yourself. You throw the basketball at the hoop with no intention of making a basket. Just chuck it at the backboard, then go get the rebound when it ricochets in an unpredictable direction. It's a great way to sharpen reaction skills.

I was working hard and doing a good job snagging unpredictable rebounds. Unfortunately, my aim sometimes was off target. A few times, instead of hitting the backboard, the basketball ricocheted off the side of Mrs. Smoot's house and made a pretty loud racket. Her ten million hoarded cats freaked out.

And Mrs. Smoot called the police. Derp!

I guess she and the cats thought they were being attacked by zombies or pelted by meteorites. Anyway, an officer showed up at my house.

He was pretty cool about the whole rico-chet thing and my poor aim, but he told me to move the basketball hoop to some other part of the backyard so that I didn't drive Mrs. Smoot and her ten million hoarded cats right out of their skulls.

I had to keep practicing my rebounding. I wasn't going to get a chance to play in a Mighty Plumbers basketball game unless I worked for it.

So after the police officer left, I rolled the portable hoop to the opposite side of my back-yard against our other neighbor's fence.

And I crossed my fingers and hoped that my off-target throws wouldn't freak out Mr. Verheyen's backyard chicken coop full of egg-laying hens.

CHAPTER 10

The Mighty Plumbers' next game was played at Stanford Middle School, home of the Green. That's their team name. A color. And it's not even plural. Just Green.

(Coach told us Stanford's nickname once was the "Raging Robins." But school officials changed it because they were worried that opponents would be frightened by the image of an enraged yard bird, which I've always thought was the whole point of a sports mascot.)

The Spiro basketball players got to skip our last-period class. Most of the team lucked out because they missed math class.

But Stephanie Jennison and I missed literature, which is one of my favorite classes—and one of the few subjects where I get above-average grades.

Ms. Katinsky teaches literature. She also teaches theater and, on the side, coaches a couple of Spiro teams in order to earn a few extra bucks to pay for personal expenses. Stuff like food and rent.

In case you don't already know, schoolteachers work hard, but they don't exactly rake in a lot of cash like other professionals.

That seems backward. If it weren't for teachers, the world would be crawling with people who can't count or spell or sit quietly at a desk all day.

I personally think the world should be more like this:

Maybe in some other universe.

Anyway, Stephanie and I skipped last period. I grabbed my basketball gear out of my locker. It was in a sports bag my dad had used when he was a hotshot athlete back in the ancient 1980s. It's an actual *leather* bag. Not one of those wimpy synthetic bags that every kid in middle school drags around.

The Spiro basketball team gathered in the parking lot and lined up to get on the van to our game across town at Stanford Middle School.

I probably don't even need to explain this,

but the primo seats on trips to away games are in the back of the van.

No players ever actually *choose* to sit up front.

Joey, Carlos, and I lined up with most of the other players at the van doorway. But Jimmy Jimerino and his kiss-up posse member, Skinny Dennis, barged past everyone and took over the primo seats in the back of the van.

Jimmy sprawled out on the back bench seat and told lame jokes loud enough for the entire van to hear. Skinny was obligated to laugh his rear end off even though he'd already heard the same jokes about a million times.

(I thought it was ironic that Jimmy would tell that particular joke.)

Meanwhile, my friends and I ended up sitting in seats next to Coach at the front of the van.

Carlos sat next to Coach Earwax. He was totally trapped into silence and non-shenanigans. Joey and I sat in the seats across the aisle so we could at least talk to each other.

On the ride to the game against the Green, I thought about leaning across the aisle and asking Coach Earwax if he could figure out some kind of rotation system for seating on van rides to away games.

But the timing wasn't right.

He was busy cleaning wax out of his brain so he'd be able to make brilliant coaching decisions during the game.

CHAPTER

In spite of their weak and useless team nickname, Stanford Middle School had one of the best basketball teams in the league.

Before running out onto the court, our team huddled around Coach Earwax in the visitors' dank locker room for his pregame pep talk.

(The visitors' locker room was musty and unsanitary, because it's practically a rule in school sports that home teams force the visiting teams to change clothes in squalid conditions.)

In our huddle, Coach told us the only way that we could defeat the Green was with a "total team effort."

Coach used that term a lot. And every time he did, he looked directly at Jimmy Jimerino.

His pep talk went on for another few minutes, but I missed much of what he said because my brain zoned out to random thoughts of lizards and cheeseburgers. My mind does that a lot, mostly when a coach or teacher or parent gets too wordy.

Anyway, I did hear one thing Coach Earwax told us. It was a quote from John Wooden, that ancient college basketball coach who Billionaire Bill also quoted.

BE QUICK, BUT DON'T HURRY!

UH...

WHAAAA???

HUH??

My teammates didn't understand, but I sort of knew what he was talking about because my mom had used a similar phrase when I was learning how to mow the lawn.

I'd rushed to get the job done so I could go do something more fun, like . . . um, pretty much anything else but mow the lawn. But because I hurried, I'd missed a bunch of little strips of grass. Then I had to go back and mow them again. Mom told me:

"The hurrier you go, the behinder you get!"

Mom meant that if I rushed the job, mistakes would be made. And I think that ancient Wooden dude was saying the same thing.

CHAPTER 12

The game against Stanford didn't begin the way Coach Earwax had hoped.

The Mighty Plumbers did not have a "total team effort." We had a "total one-man effort." Jimmy Jimerino was the star. Without the rest of the team.

Here's a short description of the first half of Spiro's basketball game against Stanford:

Jimmy. Jimmy. Jimmy.

He scored every single point in the first half. The Mighty Plumbers shuffled into the musty and unsanitary visitors' locker room trailing the Green, 50–42.

Skinny slapped Jimmy on the back and gave him high fives. Why? I don't know. You'd have to ask Skinny, who was wide open under the hoop during the entire first half because he was at least a foot taller than the Green center.

As soon as we were all inside the locker room, Coach Earwax slammed the door. He walked over to Jimmy and stuck his nose about two inches away from Jimmy's nose.

Then Coach went off on a rant that sprayed about a gallon of spit right in Jimmy's face. And I'm not even exaggerating!

I didn't catch everything that Coach Earwax yelled at Jimmy because, once again, he got really wordy and my mind zoned out to random thoughts of lizards and cheeseburgers.

But I did hear Coach asking Jimmy about

a hundred times: "Where was the team effort?" And "Is there an 'I' in team?" Oh, and "Why are you smiling?"

The entire time Coach Earwax was lecturing, Jimmy had one of those smile/smirk things going on with his mouth. Coach clearly thought it was a smile. The rest of us knew it was a smirk.

Jimmy's brain might have been just zoning out to random thoughts of cheeseburgers and lizards.

Or maybe not.

Anyway, Coach Earwax told Jimmy—right in front of the entire team—that he would be benched if his "selfishness" did not disappear in the second half.

CHAPTER 13

Jimmy did play more like a teammate in the second half. Sort of.

After the tip-off, Becky made an excellent move to get free under the basket. Jimmy wanted to shoot from WAY outside, but he tripped and had to make an awkward pass to Becky. She scored an easy layup.

After that, Jimmy relapsed. He was a ball hog and the Mighty Plumbers fell further behind.

The Green center scored six unanswered points. Even though he was shorter than Skinny, he was quick. And he wasn't selfish.

After scoring his six points, the center dished out passes to his teammates, and Stanford jumped out to a twenty-five-point lead.

The Mighty Plumbers were getting smeared by the Green.

Coach Earwax called a time-out. He took a knee in front of our bench. But he didn't scribble diagrams on his whiteboard. Coach pointed at Joey.

GO IN FOR JIMMY.

The time-out ended, and Joey entered the game as the point guard. Jimmy took a seat on the bench next to me. He was not happy. And neither was his dad.

Mr. Jimerino had to follow strict rules

when attending Mighty Plumbers games: No yelling at players. No yelling at referees. No yelling at coaches. And he had to sit right in front of our school principal, Mother T, who has a mysterious mental power that controls weak and useless parents.

But right when Jimmy sat down on the bench and Joey entered the game, Mother T left the bleachers to get a hot dog and a soda. Or maybe to go to the restroom. I don't know for sure.

Anyway, when Mother T left and Joey went into the game for Jimmy, Mr. Jimerino broke out of his disciplinary probation. He jumped up and launched into one of his notorious rants.

Quick Time-Out about Mr. Jimerino

I'm about 73 percent sure that what I know about Jimmy's dad is pretty much the truth.

My best friend Joey told me that his dad went to Spiro T. Agnew Middle School with

Mr. Jimerino way back in the ancient 1980s. They both played sports, but Joey's dad was a hotshot athlete and Jimmy's dad was a benchwarmer.

He sat on the pine in baseball, football, soccer, and basketball. The Spiro coach only put Mr. Jimerino in the game if the score was a hundred to zip.

I guess that didn't exactly fry his burger, because now Mr. Jimerino does everything he can to make sure that Jimmy is a hotshot athlete in all sports.

Mr. Jimerino is at every tryout. Every practice. Every scrimmage. Every preseason game. Every league game. Every championship game. He even tries to weasel his way into team meetings.

Before every practice or game, Mr.

LOCKER ROOM

Jimerino pulls Jimmy aside for a talk. No one knows exactly what he is saying, but we can tell that it is some kind of lecture because Jimmy's shoulders are all slumped and his head is bowed.

And during the game?

Mr. Jimerino behaves as if HE were playing in the game. Why? I don't know. You'd have to ask Mr. Jimerino. But I'm pretty sure all you'd get in response is an angry rant.

My grandfather, who is basically a hermit and lives on a sailboat in Hawaii, once told me about a mysterious mental condition where some parents "live vicariously" through their kids.

That means Mr. Jimerino pretty much feels like he got ripped off during his playing days at Spiro T. Agnew Middle School, and he's trying to make up for it through his son.

Mr. Jimerino wants to pressure his son to be the hotshot athlete that he wanted to be.

Or at least I'm 73 percent sure that's what Mr. Jimerino is thinking.

• • •

When Jimmy sat down on the pine and Joey replaced him in the game, Jimmy's dad stood up and shouted at Coach Earwax. He didn't really need to shout, though.

Coach Earwax ignored Jimmy's dad (or maybe Coach's ears were too clogged with wax to hear him), and Joey took over as the Mighty Plumbers point guard.

Then Mother T returned to her seat and Mr. Jimerino immediately went silent.

CHAPTER

14

I would love to tell you that the Mighty Plumbers basketball team suddenly woke up and played like champions when Joey hit the court, but that would be a huge whopper.

There was hope in the first minute.

Skinny Dennis passed the ball to Joey, who darted downcourt, around, through, and under the Stanford defenders.

In spite of his tiny size, Joey was quick as a flea, and the Green defense struggled to stop him from dribbling deep into the key. He was awesome!

It looked like Joey could score an easy layup, but at the last second he passed the ball to a teammate.

Skinny was wide open under the basket, but he was used to Jimmy's habit of *never* passing the ball.

Derp!

The Green point guard grabbed the rebound off of Skinny's forehead and dribbled the entire length of the court and scored an easy layup.

Mr. Jimerino, of course, blamed it all on

poor Joey. I heard him mumble, quietly, so that Mother T couldn't hear him.

When Mr. Jimerino mumbled that rude comment about my friend Joey, I got an urge to do something desperate.

We were losing by twenty-seven points. The Spiro crowd was gloomy and silent. Even the usually perky and hyperactive cheerleaders were all dreary and scrunching their faces as if someone had just cut cheese.

I decided to do the Rally Slide.

It was a huge risk. I had no idea if it could actually change the momentum of a game or if it was just a fluke. I could look like a fool for absolutely no reason. But I was sitting on the bench and didn't really have much else to do.

I waited until the Mighty Plumbers had possession of the ball. Joey was standing at the top of the key preparing to do his quick-as-a-flea dash to the hoop.

I got up and imagined that a gym rat had just stolen a tasty protein bar from Ricky Schnauzer's neatly stacked pile and it was making a break for its hideout under the bleachers.

I took three steps, dove onto my belly, and slid ten feet across the floor like a baseball player diving to snag a line drive.

Fortunately, the Spiro fans in the bleachers behind our bench remembered my epic belly slide in the game against the Chaney Werewolves. They all jumped up and down and cheered.

All except one.

THERE'S SOMETHING WRONG WITH THAT BOY.

Joey and the other Mighty Plumbers on the court heard the burst of cheers from the Spiro crowd, and it pumped up their spirits.

Becky darted to the top of the key and set a pick for Joey. (A pick is sort of like a block in football, except no one gets their bones broken or face smashed into the ground.)

Becky's pick allowed Joey to dribble around the key to the baseline, close to the basket. Instead of taking a shot, Joey passed the ball back to Becky. Then she passed the ball to Dewey, who passed the ball to Stephanie, who passed the ball to Skinny, who scored.

Every player on our team played a part in scoring the basket!

The Spiro crowd started chanting:

"Rally Slide! Rally Slide! Rally Slide!"

So I did it again.

I took three steps, dove onto my belly, and slid ten feet across the floor. And that's all it took. The Mighty Plumbers seized the Big Mo.

With Jimmy sitting on the bench in the final minutes, the Mighty Plumbers rallied from a twenty-seven-point deficit and defeated the Stanford Green by two points.

Joey did a great job filling in at point guard, but there were no stars in the comeback win. It was a team effort. Even I got credit.

KEEP DOING THAT BELLY SLIDE THING!!

I was going to tell Coach about the felonious gym rat that stole expensive protein bars, but Jimmy approached Coach Earwax with his head bowed. It looked like he was maybe going to apologize for hogging the ball, so I gave them some privacy.

But before Jimmy even said a word to Coach, Mr. Jimerino swooped in and pulled his son away.

The team got on the van for the ride to Spiro T. Agnew Middle School. But Jimmy was not on board.

Jimmy road home with his dad. Meanwhile, two others took over his prime shenanigans seat in the back of the van.

Becky and *Ricky*?!
Oh. My. Derp.

CHAPTER 15

The day after our win against the Stanford Green, I took my basketball out into the backyard for more rebounding practice.

I was happy that our team had won. And my Rally Slide had turned into a fun sideline attraction that may or may not have helped Spiro regain the Big Mo.

But my mind was set on getting off the bench and into the game. I knew there was something more I could do to contribute. So I went back to work to become a lean, mean rebounding machine.

I had already moved my portable basketball hoop to the side of the yard away from Mrs. Smoot and her ten million hoarded cats, which were scared out of their tiny brains by any kind of loud noise.

The hoop was set up next to my other neighbor's fence.

The chickens in Mr. Verheyen's backyard were really laid-back. They pretty much just pecked at mysterious edible stuff in the grass all day and then laid eggs in a henhouse at night.

I was worried that my rebounding noise would disturb the hens and they would freak out and quit laying eggs. But Mr. Verheyen's chickens didn't even flinch.

I threw the basketball at the backboard, intentionally missing the hoop, and then I grabbed the rebound. And I kept doing it, over and over, until it was dark and Mr. Verheyen's chickens had gone home to roost.

I was determined to become a lean, mean rebounding machine.

CHAPTER 16

The Mighty Plumbers' next game was at home versus Simplot Middle School. At the start of the season, sports pundits predicted that the Blazing Spuds would struggle in a "rebuilding year."

That's a polite way of saying the Simplot basketball team was weak and useless and they would get creamed in every game.

Most of the time, everything that sports pundits say ends up being wrong. Then they slink off and hide in a closet full of stanky socks until they reemerge the next season when everyone has forgotten all about their failed guesswork. Then they make wrong predictions all over again.

But this season, the sports pundits had blindly stumbled onto a correct prediction. The Blazing Spuds really were a weak and useless team.

With a goofy-looking mascot.

As usual, Becky, Dewey, Stephanie, and Skinny started the game against the Blazing Spuds. But Jimmy? There was a consequence for hogging the ball in the game against the Stanford Green.

Coach Earwax suspended Jimmy for the

first quarter of the game, which I guess was better than no consequence at all.

Mr. Jimerino was in the bleachers, sitting right in front of our school principal. Mother T sat with her hands folded on her lap, and Mr. Jimerino kept his mouth closed for the entire game.

Joey started at point guard. He had the entire first quarter all to himself, and he didn't waste a single minute of the opportunity.

Joey darted like a flea around and under the Blazing Spuds defense. Then he passed the ball off to teammates who were wide open. Joey didn't score, but he did get twenty assists in a single quarter!

The Mighty Plumbers were ahead, 40–16, when Joey sat down on the pine and Jimmy entered the game at the start of the second quarter.

Jimmy seemed to have changed his hotshot attitude. When he jumped off the bench, Jimmy shoved his water bottle into my hands and told me to hold it for him.

But then he added:

PLEASE.

Whoa.

I had never heard hotshot athlete Jimmy or any of his kiss-up posse say that word. Ever.

Instead of hogging the ball, Jimmy played like a true point guard. He controlled the ball and passed the ball and took a shot only if no one else was open.

It was a total team effort. The Mighty Plumbers pretty much smeared the weak and useless Blazing Spuds.

I sat the pine for the entire game, even

though there was never a need for me to do the Rally Slide to change the momentum.

Why? I don't know. You'd have to ask Coach Earwax.

But I almost did a Rally Slide for a reason other than the Big Mo.

That felonious gym rat tried to help itself to another tasty and expensive protein bar. But when it poked its head out from under the bleachers, I turned and spotted it.

I think the rat must have recognized me from the first game of the season. It ducked back under the bleachers and never returned.

The highlight of our victory over the Spuds, however, didn't even happen during the game.

After the game, before we all went into the locker room to change, Dewey picked up a basketball and launched a jump shot. It's sort of his postgame ritual. He won't leave the court until he makes a hoop.

But this time he didn't make the shot or

miss the shot. It was sort of in between.

The basketball bounced around the rim and then settled, perfectly balanced, on the bracket between the rim and backboard.

Everyone took turns trying to knock it down. Becky, Jimmy, Stephanie, Skinny, Jimmy, Carlos, me—even Ricky Schnauzer. We all failed, although I only missed it by a fraction of an inch.

Finally, Ricky fetched a broom. He was just about to poke the basketball loose with the broom handle when Joey literally sprang into action.

You already know that Joey is quick as a flea. But we all found out he also can *jump* like a flea.

The smallest guy on the Mighty Plumbers team walked underneath the basketball hoop. Then he jumped straight up—ten feet. Wow!

And I'm not even making that up!

CHAPTER

So this has nothing to do with basketball or the Rally Slide or my obsessive quest to become a lean, mean rebounding machine. But I need to bring something up that's really awkward.

And I already know what you're going to say.

YOU ASKED BECKY TO THE FALL DANCE AND SHE SCORCHED YOU!

RANDOM KID IN THE CROWD

No!

Well, yes. Sort of.

I did ask Becky to the dance. But she didn't technically "scorch me," so don't even think that, okay? She had a previous commitment.

I probably shouldn't have waited until the day before the Fall Dance to ask Becky, but that bad habit is common among guys my age.

Well, most guys my age.

Ricky Schnauzer had asked Becky two weeks—*two weeks*—before the Fall Dance!

So when I finally mustered up the nerve to ask Becky in the hallway between history class and geography class, I was way too late. She had no choice but to turn me down because Becky would never back out on Ricky or anyone else after she had already said yes.

It was nothing personal. And I wasn't the only one who Becky turned down.

Jimmy also had waited to ask Becky until

the day before the Fall Dance. He asked her about thirty seconds after I got scorched . . . er, turned down by Becky.

Jimmy didn't handle it very well.

RICKY SCHNAUZER? TWO WEEKS AGO?!

I had estimated my chances of a positive response from Becky to be about 70 percent, which is pretty much the score I get on every math test. But Jimmy probably figured his chance for a Fall Dance date with Becky was 100 percent.

I think he had assumed that Becky would blow off all other requests so that she could accept an invitation from Spiro's hotshot athlete and Big Jock on Campus.

But Jimmy quickly recovered from his meltdown and went to his B Plan.

Once again, he was about thirty seconds too late.

Right after Becky turned me down, as I was walking to geography class, Stephanie tapped me on my shoulder.

When I turned around, she was holding up a sheet of binder paper with the words "Will you be my date?" written in perfect Sharpie penmanship.

She apparently had the same day-before-the-dance bad habit as most guys my age.

Anyway, I had a date for the Fall Dance. And I didn't even have to muster up any nerve to ask Stephanie!

About thirty seconds later, right after I told Stephanie that I would go to the dance with her, Jimmy strolled up and moved between me and Stephanie.

I turned and made a quick dash for geography class. Behind me I heard Jimmy's response to getting scorched by Stephanie.

"You asked *Steve Moore?!* . . . *Thirty seconds* ago?!!"

CHAPTER 18

A couple of hours before the Fall Dance, I took my basketball out into the backyard to work on my quest to become a lean, mean rebounding machine.

The Mighty Plumbers had a game the next night, and I wanted to be ready in case I got a chance to get off the bench and show Coach Earwax my skills.

I started chucking the basketball at the portable backboard next to the fence between

my house and Mr. Verheyen's. About five minutes later, he poked his head above the fence
and motioned for me to come over.

I thought Mr. Verheyen was going to
demand that I stop annoying his chickens or
inform me that he had called the police. But
I was wrong.

Fresh eggs! It was a gift.

Apparently, all the racket I had been making in previous rebounding practices had
triggered a psychological effect on his chickens that boosted their production. He now
had more eggs than he and his entire family
and close circle of friends could use.

I worked on my rebounding skills for

another hour, then decided to quit. My big Fall Dance date with Stephanie was getting close, and I didn't want to get so sweaty that even a shower couldn't wash away the corrosive middle-schooler perspiration.

But I just couldn't resist tossing the basketball at the backboard one more time. The ball bounced off the rim and flew toward the basket of eggs from Mr. Verheyen, which I had stupidly set on the ground nearby.

I dove for the rebound to save the eggs. But when I landed, my face smacked into a ceramic garden gnome that my mom had bought at a neighborhood garage sale in a moment of weakness.

Not even one of the eggs got cracked. And the garden gnome survived.

But I ended up with a big, swollen, gnarly black eye.

One hour before the Fall Dance.

CHAPTER

My turbo-hyper-worrywart mom made me hold an ice pack against my eye right up until I left for the dance. She was worried that it would swell completely shut and my date would be grossed out and not want to be seen with me.

But Dad said the black eye made me look "tough." Like a hotshot hockey player after a nasty bench-clearing brawl.

I looked in the mirror one more time. After

an hour under the ice pack, the swelling had gone down a little.

I couldn't tell if the eye looked gross or tough or like an eye that had slammed into a ceramic garden gnome.

My dad drove me to Spiro. Stephanie and I had arranged to meet under the giant Mighty Plumbers mural in the cafeteria, which is where the dance was held.

At Spiro T. Agnew Middle School, it's practically a rule that no one rides with a mom or dad to pick up a date at their home.

It's too awkward. You don't know whether to sit in the back seat with the date, like in a taxi, or split up and sit in front with your parent. Anyway, I'd rather wait until I'm old enough to get my hands on the wheel of a Porsche 911 Turbo and pick up the date by myself.

When I walked into the cafeteria, it was pretty obvious that everyone else had told their dates to meet them under the Mighty Plumbers mural. There was a big crowd of kids standing around waiting in two separate groups. Guys in one; girls in the other.

My two best guy friends were there. Joey was wearing a dress shirt with a hand-me-down tie from one of his older brothers. It was a little big.

Carlos also was wearing a tie—with a *T-shirt*. Why? I don't know, but that's just Carlos.

I looked for Stephanie. She hadn't arrived yet, so I wandered over to the guys group and stuck my hands in my pockets like everyone else and tried to act cool and nonchalant.

That was impossible to pull off, though, because I had a big, honking black eye.

Carlos was the first to spot my shiner. Or at least he was the first to say something about it in a really loud voice.

Good ol' Carlos. At least he didn't belch-speak the sentence, but it was almost just as loud.

Both groups—guys and girls—gathered

around me to check out my eye. But they weren't concerned about things like, oh, whether I'd permanently lost my vision. They all had *way* more important questions.

Dewey Taylor actually ran out of the cafeteria when he saw my black eye because it brought back gory memories of the time a baseball slammed into his face and smashed his nose sideways and gave him *two* black eyes.

I tried to concoct a story that didn't include the ceramic garden gnome, but before I could make up some kind of gigantic whopper, my date arrived.

Stephanie Jennison wore a black dress

and had on heels, which made her about two inches taller than me.

She walked over and sort of leaned down for a close look at my black eye. I just stood there in silence with hands in my pockets and braced myself for what she might say in front of everybody.

After a few seconds, Stephanie smiled and broke the ice.

After that, everyone finally began pairing off with their dates.

Joey had been asked to the dance by Liz Casey, the student body president. She had a gigantic crush on Joey ever since soccer season. Liz is very popular and a good student, but she has a speech habit that drives every-one at Spiro right out of their skulls:

All of Liz's sentences end in a question mark. No periods. No exclamation points. Just question marks.

Carlos's date was Jessica Whitehead, the school genius. She and Carlos sort of had "a thing" back in football season that didn't last very long, but apparently they had decided to give it another shot. Things got off to a rocky start, though.

I already mentioned that Ricky Schnauzer was the basketball team's equipment manager. He's very neat and organized. Everything about Ricky is impeccably planned. Perfectly timed. And his entrance to the Fall Dance with Becky O'Callahan was no exception.

Ricky and Becky pulled up in front of school in a shiny black limousine. And it wasn't driven by a mom or a dad or a sullen older brother. The driver was an actual professional chauffeur.

At the very instant that the music in the cafeteria started and the spotlights turned on, the basketball team's equipment manager and the best athlete at Spiro T. Agnew Middle School (with Nature's Near-Perfect Smile) walked into the cafeteria.

Side by side. Arm in arm. Ricky in a tuxedo—*a tuxedo*! Becky in a full-length formal dress.

And their hair was perfect.

Wow.

In one well-planned instant, Ricky Schnauzer raised the bar impossibly high for every weak and useless guy with a date at the Spiro T. Agnew Middle School annual Fall Dance.

CHAPTER 20

Carlos and Jessica broke off their attempt to revive "a thing" about ten minutes into the Fall Dance. The hotshot school genius expected Carlos to bow to her every wish. But Carlos was a little confused about the whole Fall Dance concept.

WAIT. WHAT? NO ONE TOLD ME I'D HAVE TO DANCE!...HEY, I CAN CHANGE!!

Meanwhile, Joey played hard to get.

STOP RUNNING.? I CAN'T KEEP UP?!

Stephanie and I got along pretty well, though. Maybe even really well, but don't even make too much of that, okay?

It's not like we were "a thing." But she was fun. Oh, and she smelled good. How did I know? Because we danced to a slow song.

Quick Time-Out about Dancing

I'm one of those people who have a hard time dancing.

Fast dance or medium dance or slow dance. I pretty much just try to fake it. But the hardest to fake is a fast dance because it takes physical and mental coordination.

I've already told you that, even though I'm a benchwarmer, I do have some skills that involve coordination. But dancing to a fast song is not one of them.

I have Upbeat-O-Phobia, which is a morbid fear of dancing to a fast song.

I'm not a total drooling dweeb dancer. So don't even think that, okay? But I can't dance to upbeat songs that require more than one of my muscle groups to move in coordination with the music.

I always end up looking something like this:

But I can handle a slow dance. It's easy. You sort of just hang on to your partner and sway from side to side.

By the way, it's pretty much a strict rule that you don't look directly at your partner during a slow dance. Look at the floor or the ceiling or the Mighty Plumbers mural on the wall. Look at anything other than your dance partner.

Oh, and talking while slow dancing is frowned upon, so keep your mouth shut.

Unless you feel like telling her that she smells good.

● ● ●

Becky and Ricky danced to every song—fast, medium, and slow. They looked at each other while dancing. They talked to each other while dancing. And I'm not even making that up.

It wasn't like I was keeping track or anything. Maybe a little. But everyone else was keeping track, too.

I know Becky pretty well. Joey, Carlos, Becky, and I hang out a lot. We're teammates in school sports and we hang out at Goodfellow Stadium to watch professional sports. And, of course, Becky and I share a love of nature's near-perfect food—Eskimo Pies!

So I know that Becky would never dance with Ricky to every song unless it fried her burger. It didn't matter to Becky that he was a finicky team equipment manager and not a hotshot athlete star of the Mighty Plumbers basketball team.

And that is why everyone at Spiro T. Agnew Middle School likes Becky O'Callahan.

Halfway through the Fall Dance, Jimmy Jimerino walked into the cafeteria along with a couple of members of his kiss-up posse. They didn't have dates, but there were some other students there without dates so they didn't have to stand around with hands in their pockets and not dance.

Not that it mattered to Jimmy.

In the last basketball game, he seemed to have overcome his hotshot entitlement attitude. But apparently, he had relapsed, because instead of asking a girl who did not have a date to dance, he asked Becky O'Callahan.

Becky and Ricky were right in the middle of a conversation, but Jimmy didn't care. He just walked up to Becky and said, "Let's dance!"

She wasn't interested, though. Becky didn't even respond. Instead, she took Ricky by the hand and led him out onto the dance floor.

Jimmy watched them walk away, then shrugged and looked around the cafeteria. His next target was Stephanie, but my date didn't even let him get close enough to ask her to dance.

Jimmy walked toward her, flashing his hotshot smile. But Stephanie held up both of her hands, palms out like a traffic cop, and he made a quick U-turn.

It wasn't a good night for Jimmy. But he did manage to dance with one girl who had come to the Fall Dance with a date.

Stephanie and I had a great time. Normally, I have a hard time talking to girls, but Stephanie and I talked the whole night except when one of us had to go to the restroom. In fact, we even broke a couple of rules when we danced to a slow song.

CHAPTER

The Mighty Plumbers' next game was at
D. B. Cooper Middle School, Home of the
Leaping Lizards.

GROWLLLL...

Since it was an away game, the team members skipped last period and filed onto the van for the ride. Joey, Carlos, and I sat up front in the seats next to Coach because we assumed that Jimmy would hog the back seat.

But Jimmy didn't even show up for the van ride.

Coach Earwax had the van driver wait in the parking lot just in case Jimmy was delayed by a teacher or he got dizzy and disoriented and couldn't find the parking lot.

After waiting about ten minutes, Coach told the van driver to close the doors, and we left for the game. When we arrived at D. B. Cooper Middle School, Jimmy was waiting for us. He had ridden to the game with his dad.

Mr. Jimerino tried to talk to Coach Earwax when he got off the van, but Coach pretended to be digging for earwax with his car key and walked past him without saying a word.

I was pretty confident that I would get in the game against the Leaping Lizards. I had been doing all of the extra rebounding work in the backyard, throwing the ball against the hoop next to Mr. Verheyen's super chill chickens.

And in team practices, the hard work had paid off. I'd grabbed more rebounds than anyone else on the team, including Skinny Dennis. Coach Earwax even gave me pretty much the highest compliment a player can get from any coach in the entire world.

ATTA BABE STEVE!!

I didn't start the Leaping Lizards game, though. I didn't even play for one second.

The Leaping Lizards played what Coach

called "small ball." Their players weren't very big, but they were speedy and shifty.

On offense, they were constantly in motion and passed the ball to one another, around the key, until a player got wide open for a shot. And their quick hands on defense created turnovers.

Skinny was about a foot taller than D. B. Cooper's tallest player, but he was slower. He had a hard time keeping up with the small ballers. They buzzed around him like mosquitos.

Jimmy, Becky, Dewey, and Stephanie also struggled on defense. They hurried to keep up with the pace. But the hurrier they went, the behinder they got.

The one bright moment was when Dewey blocked a shot and launched the basketball twenty-three rows up into the bleachers.

The Spiro fans jumped up and cheered— even Mr. Jimerino. He risked breaking his disciplinary probation, but Mother T cut him some slack because it really was an excellent blocked shot.

But the Leaping Lizards small-ballers jumped out to a ten-point lead in the first quarter.

In a huddle on the sidelines before the start of the second quarter, Coach Earwax didn't even draw mysterious diagrams on his little whiteboard. He just gave the team a short pep talk and repeated that quote from the ancient 1970s basketball coach.

BE QUICK.
BUT DON'T HURRY...

After the Mighty Plumbers starting five jogged out onto the court for the second quarter, Coach motioned for me to come over to him. I was hoping he was going to tell me to be ready to go in the game on a second's notice, but that didn't happen.

Coach Earwax whispered in my ear.

"Do that belly thingy. You know. The Rally Slide."

I would have preferred to have gone into the game to do my excellent rebound thing. But shortly after the second quarter started, I got up off the bench and did the Rally Slide.

The Spiro fans went wild. (Except Mr. Jimerino, who was still all weirded out by the Rally Slide.)

And when the Mighty Plumbers on the

court saw the Rally Slide and heard the Spiro fans cheer, they busted loose.

Becky stole an inbounds pass. Skinny scored an easy layup. Dewey blocked another shot twenty-three rows into the bleachers. Stephanie hit a three-pointer. And Jimmy?

Well, Jimmy relapsed again.

After Becky dished a pass to a wide-open Skinny for an easy score, Jimmy took over. Once again, it became the Jimmy Jimerino Show.

Skinny, Becky, Dewey, and Stephanie were pretty much just bored bystanders. If basketball trunks had pockets, their hands would have been stuffed inside.

Jimmy scored nearly every one of the Mighty Plumbers' points and ignored nearly every one of the opportunities to pass the ball to a teammate who was wide open for an easy shot.

Mr. Jimerino sat, tall and proud, in his bleacher seat and smiled.

Joey, Carlos, and I sat on the bench and

watched. We were even more bored than the starters playing with Jimmy. Our minds wandered.

It was the perfect time to pull off one of our famous bench pranks to entertain ourselves and mess with the opposing team.

Quick Time-Out about Bench Pranks

One of our favorites is to prank-call the coach of the opposing team right in the middle of the game.

It's easy to get the coach's cell-phone number. We just ask one of his or her players during warm-ups when everyone's loosening up and trying to act all cool.

If you play basketball, you know what I'm talking about. All the players strut around the court before the game, dribbling between their legs and trying to look like NBA prospects.

So if I happen to meet an opposing

player at half-court, there is an exchange of small talk that might go something like this:

Me: "Hey."

Weak and useless opponent: "Hey. Where'd ya get that gnarly black eye?"

Me: "Hockey fight."

Weak and useless opponent: "Cool."

Me: "Whaddaya play?"

Weak and useless opponent: "Point guard."

Me: "Cool."

Weak and useless opponent: "Whaddaya play?"

Me: "Rally Slider."

Weak and useless opponent: "Um . . ."

Then I cleverly pry the number out of his weak and useless mind.

Me: "What's your coach's private cell-phone number?"

And they spill the beans every single time.

Joey, Carlos, and I wait until a crucial

moment of the game. Like maybe in the final seconds when the score is tied and the opposing coach is trying to think up a brilliant strategy.

Carlos always makes the call because he can bottle up air in his gut and fake a deep adult voice. When the coach answers, Carlos says, "Congratulations! You've just won TEN MILLION DOLLARS!"

. . . If the coach can answer one simple question: "Who was the inventor of dental floss?"

It's a brain stumper that momentarily distracts the coach from the crucial moment in the game.

The prank victims rarely even make a guess, although one coach actually answered "LeBron James," which probably isn't correct.

• • •

Unfortunately, the three Benchkateers couldn't pull off that prank even though I had cleverly pried the coach's private cell number out of a weak and useless Leaping Lizards player.

When Carlos called the number, it went direct to voice mail.

"I CAN'T PICK UP RIGHT NOW...
I'M TRYING TO THINK UP A BRILLIANT
STRATEGY... LEAVE A MESSAGE
AND I WILL GET BACK TO YOU!!"

Derp!

The three Benchkateers sat on our rear ends for the rest of the game and drank Gatorade for no reason because we'd done exactly nothing to deplete our vital body fluids.

Jimmy (er, the Mighty Plumbers) creamed the Leaping Lizards small-ballers by about forty points. After many close calls and epic comebacks, we had somehow achieved a perfect record for the season, with one game remaining. If we won, Spiro would be in the championship game against the top team from the other division in our league.

Everyone except Jimmy got on the van for the ride back to Spiro T. Agnew Middle School. Coach Earwax and the entire team watched Jimmy and his dad get into their car and drive out of the parking lot.

Joey and I saw Coach Earwax scribble something in his top-secret clipboard. Joey craned his neck, trying to see what he'd written, but Coach flipped the clipboard upside down and stashed it in his bag.

During the trip back to Spiro, Skinny stood up and started a chant:

"Undefeated! Undefeated! Undefeated!"

Everyone on the van joined in the chant— even the van driver.

I wondered if our perfect-record chant would jinx us—like in baseball when a pitcher has a no-hitter going and no one can mention it out loud or it'll ruin everything.

I was sitting next to Coach Earwax, so I asked him about the jinx. Coach yanked a few nose hairs out of a nostril (another of his gross habits). Then he told me that basketball is immune to baseball superstitions.

With one exception.

"In baseball, they have inside-out Rally Caps. It works just like your amazing Rally Slide!"

I had a feeling I would be sitting on the bench in the upcoming games. Ready in an instant to play my crucial team role if the Mighty Plumbers need to regain the Big Mo.

Um, derp.

CHAPTER 22

The next day, I got back to practicing rebounds.

I went into the backyard and was about to throw my basketball repeatedly against the backboard so that I could become a lean, mean rebounding machine.

Before I even made one throw, I was interrupted by a familiar but annoying commotion.

My psychotic poodle, Frenchy, was pawing

frantically at the sliding-glass door. He had emerged from his "doghouse" underneath my bed because his bladder was about to explode. He needed to get outside in a hurry.

I let Frenchy out into the backyard, but that just caused another commotion.

Frenchy bolted to the grass next to our pond to do his business. Cleo, my pet duck who thinks she is a dog, waddled out of the pond and tried to make out with Frenchy even though she doesn't even have lips.

Cleo is head over webbed feet in love with Frenchy. Unfortunately, she doesn't exactly fry Frenchy's burger. Not even close.

Frenchy is pretty much a cranky hermit, unless he wants food or water or access to the backyard to do his business.

The two pets got into a beak/snout lovers' quarrel.

I had to set my basketball down and go break it up.

Cleo jumped back into the pond and pouted, which is really hard to do if you don't have lips. Frenchy went back into the house, crawled underneath my bed, and did whatever psychotic poodles do when they're all alone.

I picked up the basketball and launched into my rebounding drill. Toss and rebound. Toss and rebound. Toss and rebound.

It was getting dark, but I kept going. I needed to get better so that I could earn my way into the lineup. (And I knew it would motivate Mr. Verheyen's super-chill chickens next door to crank out more delicious eggs.)

My dad came out into the backyard and told me to come inside because dinner was ready. He asked me why I had moved the backboard next to Mr. Verheyen's fence.

I told him that I'd moved the backboard away from Mrs. Smoot's hoard of demented cats because she'd called the police.

After Dad got over a laughing fit, he asked why I was out of breath and soaked in corrosive middle-schooler sweat. (I don't think he was worried about the sweat damaging any nearby structures, though. He was just curious.)

I told Dad that I wanted to become a lean, mean rebounding machine and work my way into the Mighty Plumbers lineup, but so far it wasn't exactly working out. Then I spilled the beans about the felonious gym rat and the accidental Rally Slide that had doomed me to permanent bench duty.

He started another laughing fit, but Dad

cut it short because he could tell that I was bummed out about not getting in games.

"You're doing the right thing. Keep working hard. It'll pay off."

Dad asked for the basketball. The former hotshot athlete probably hadn't touched a basketball since the ancient 1980s, but he walked to the opposite side of the yard next to Mrs. Smoot's fence and launched a jump shot all the way back across the yard toward the hoop.

Nothing but net!

Dad turned and walked into the house as if it was no big deal.

I was both amazed and discouraged.

CHAPTER 23

Our final regular season game was against the Madmen of A. E. Neuman Middle School.

Stephanie and I skipped Ms. Katinsky's literature class and retrieved our sports bags from our lockers. Then we walked out to the parking lot to board the van.

Both the Mighty Plumbers and the Madmen were undefeated and tied for the division lead. Coach Earwax had prepared us for a hard-fought game. We were focused and determined—even Ricky Schnauzer, who had the fragrant towels, water bottles, and tasty protein bars neatly stacked and stored in the back of the van.

Stephanie sat up front with me, Joey, and Carlos. Becky sat in the middle of the van next to Ricky, who was dressed in a pressed collared shirt and slacks. His hair was perfect.

In the back of the van, Dewey and Skinny sat in two of the three prime shenanigan seats.

Jimmy was a no-show. Again.

Coach Earwax was about to get into the van when Jimmy walked out of school carrying his game bag and Mr. Jimerino's car pulled into the parking lot. Coach motioned for Jimmy to come over to the van.

Those of us in the van didn't even have to strain to hear the conversation. Coach spoke out loud and clear.

He told Jimmy that he wanted everyone

to ride in the van together. As a team. And if Jimmy didn't do that, he would no longer be on the team.

Coach Earwax asked Jimmy if he was going to get in the van. Jimmy glanced back over his shoulder toward his dad waiting in the car. Then he shook his head.

Coach got in the van. And that was it. Jimmy was off the team.

As we pulled out of the parking lot, I looked back at Jimmy. He just stood there with his bag and watched his teammates drive off to play a game that would determine if Spiro T. Agnew Middle School would go to the Big Game.

CHAPTER 24

I was hoping the Mighty Plumbers would slaughter the weak and useless Madmen— from opening tip-off to final horn—so that I wouldn't be held back on the pine in case we needed the Rally Slide to regain the Big Mo.

But that didn't happen.

The Madmen were not weak and useless. They obviously had worked hard and prepared for the game. Even their equipment manager had the team's essential supplies neatly stacked at the end of their bench. (Her hair wasn't perfect, but pretty close.)

Meanwhile, the Mighty Plumbers struggled to adjust to the loss of our hotshot star, who'd hogged (er, scored) most of our points.

Joey took over for Jimmy at point guard. And he did a great job of controlling the ball.

Joey was quick as a flea, as usual. The Madmen had a hard time keeping him from either stealing the ball or darting through the defense and dishing off to wide-open teammates.

But the other Mighty Plumbers had never really adjusted to playing with an unselfish point guard.

One time, Joey dribbled around . . .

. . . er, *under* a defender and dished the ball off to Dewey, who was standing right under the hoop.

Just like Skinny in the other game, Dewey was not expecting the pass. He wasn't even looking.

BOOF!!

At least, it didn't hit Dewey in his schnoz.

The Madmen grabbed the turnover and scored.

On the bench, Carlos and I were hopeful that we might get in the game, but the Madmen and the Mighty Plumbers stayed within a few points of each other all the way until the end of the fourth quarter.

Finally, with only a few minutes left in the game, Coach Earwax turned and pointed at me. At first, I thought he was motioning for me to go into the game. But then he pointed at the floor and I knew what he wanted me to do.

Rally Slide.

Once again, I slid ten feet on my belly like a baseball player diving to snag a line drive. The Spiro fans jumped to their feet and cheered. And the game momentum changed.

The Mighty Plumbers played unselfish basketball and defeated the Madmen.

Spiro was headed to the league championship.

On the way to the van, Becky and Stephanie walked on either side of me and wrapped their arms over my shoulders. They could tell I was disappointed about not playing and wanted to make me feel like the Rally Slide was a big contribution.

Becky said, "Excellent Rally Slide, Steve."

And Stephanie added, "Yeah. We needed that."

That made me feel better.

But I still would rather have played in the game and grabbed about a hundred rebounds.

CHAPTER 25

The next day, I had two choices: Keep working on my rebounding skills or bag it and just slug out in my bedroom and reorganize my sports memorabilia collection.

My chances of playing in the Big Game were puny.

So I decided to devote my day off to reorganizing my collection of balls, jerseys, socks, helmets, and jocks that were signed (to the best of my knowledge) by the hotshot professional athletes who once owned them.

But then I noticed that the lid to Fido's terrarium was cockeyed. I looked inside. My snake had escaped—for about the billionth time.

At first, I thought that Fido might be roaming around the house, but I hadn't left my bedroom door open. So I searched my bedroom.

I didn't need to look under my bed because it was obvious that Frenchy was there, sound asleep. If Fido was under my bed, the psychotic poodle would be disturbed . . .

ZZZ ... FOOLS ... DESTROY THE WORLD ... ZZZZ

. . . even more than usual.

I looked in my closet under the pile of unwashed and toxic athletic socks that could have spontaneously combusted at any moment.

Nothing.

Then I spotted the rear half of Fido's body. The front half of the snake was deep into my leather sports bag.

Why was he nosing around in my bag? I don't know. You'd have to ask Fido, but good luck getting even one word out of his mouth.

Fido was overdue to be fed, so maybe he was hungry and had sniffed out the tasty protein bar in my bag that I had never got around to eating during the Madmen game.

Anyway, when I stashed Fido back in his cage I noticed that the lid was bent up as if a large reptile had repeatedly shoved his nose against it. That was Fido's escape route.

I grabbed a basketball shoe that (I'm pretty sure) was signed by Kobe Bryant and set it on top of the lid so that Fido would not shove it open and roam the earth.

Fido had escaped his cage about a billion times, and every time, he got caught and put back in the cage. But he never gave up.

His obsessive goal inspired me to go into the backyard and practice rebounds.

I tossed the basketball against the backboard and grabbed rebounds. Over and over. Until it was dark and Mr. Verheyen's chickens went back in their coop and started making eggs.

CHAPTER 26

At basketball practice before the Big Game, Jimmy walked into Spiro's dump of a gym.

But he didn't stroll in like God's gift to basketball.

Jimmy walked up to Coach Earwax with his head lowered. Then he waited patiently until Coach was done digging wax out of his ear with a car key.

I'M SORRY.

We were all expecting Coach Earwax to cave in and once again give hotshot athlete Jimmy a pass for life and let him back on the team with minimal consequences.

Coach Earwax did allow Jimmy to rejoin the team, but on one condition: He would have to plant his rear end on the bench. Permanently.

Jimmy didn't even hesitate.

"Thank you!"

On the day of the Big Game, I got up and ate breakfast. (Bacon and two eggs from the super-chill chickens next door!)

I got ready for school, then grabbed my backpack and sports bag. Then I noticed that the lid to Fido's cage was bent up and the Kobe Bryant shoe was on the floor.

Fido was gone.

There was not enough time to mount a search, so I made sure my bedroom door was closed so Fido would not roam around the house and drive my mom right out of her skull.

The league championship game was at home against Nike Preparatory Academy, home of the Platypuses. They are Spiro T. Agnew's major nemesis in every sport except baseball.

Nike is weak and useless in baseball. They're still trying to catch up.

But Nike's teams excel in every other sport because a wealthy alumni donor gives billions of dollars a year to the athletic program.

The Platypuses pulled into our parking lot, but they were not riding in a van.

It was a tour bus—one of those shiny rock-star tour buses with a kitchen and bunk beds and TV monitors and a delicious buffet and free Wi-Fi and a restroom that smells fresh and minty.

The Nike Prep bus was huge. It transported nine players, the athletic director, the head coach, four assistant coaches, three athletic trainers, an equipment manager, an assistant equipment manager, a sports information director, and a videographer with a sound technician.

And they probably could have squeezed in the Nike Prep cheerleaders, dance squad, school principal, mascot, and assistant mascot. But *they* all rode in a *second* rock-star tour bus!

(FYI: Spiro's wimpy van barely holds eight players, a coach, an athletic trainer, and a finicky equipment manager. And it struggles to get up steep hills.)

The Platypuses basketball players disembarked from their luxury ride, led by the school's athletic director. I remembered him from previous games with Nike Prep.

Jimmy Jimerino had given him the nickname "Jeeves."

Jeeves handed each player a surgical mask as they headed into the musty visitors' locker room in Spiro T. Agnew Middle School's dump of a gymnasium.

JUST A PRECAUTION.

SURGICAL MASKS

In the Mighty Plumbers locker room, we dressed for the game. I was about to stash my sports bag in my locker when I noticed water puddled inside.

I looked up. Right above my locker, water was dripping from a leak in one of our dump-of-a-gym's ancient pipes.

I couldn't leave my leather bag in the locker, where it would get soaked and turn moldy. I took it with me when the team went onto the court, and then I stashed it under the bench.

CHAPTER 27

Before the tip-off of the Big Game, Spiro fans and Nike Prep fans exchanged lame cheers.

"We've got spirit! Yes we do! We've got spirit! How 'bout you!"

"We've got MORE!!"

The two team mascots faced off on the sideline and did that typical mascot thing where they faked like they were engaged in mortal combat.

In the bleachers, Mother T took her usual
seat a few rows up behind our bench and
folded her hands on her lap. But Mr. Jimerino's seat in front of her was empty. He had
been banned.

It was the first time in the history of Spiro
T. Agnew athletics that a parent had been
banished from a basketball game!

My parents were at the game, so I looked
back and scanned the bleachers. Even in
Spiro T. Agnew's dump of a gymnasium, the
league championship game was sold out. But
I didn't need to look far, because Mom and
Dad were sitting in the seats right behind
Mother T. Derp!

Amazingly, the Spiro gym's ancient

climate-control system was not malfunction-
ing. It wasn't hot and it wasn't cold. Somehow,
Mr. Joseph, the building maintenance super-
visor, had finally come up with a fix.

Coach Earwax called us all into a huddle.
He told the starters to "be quick, but don't
hurry."

Then he pointed at me and Carlos and
said, "Be ready."

And finally, Coach pointed at the third
Spiro benchwarmer.

Jimmy Jimerino.

Carlos, Steve, and *Jimmy*. The three Benchkateers!

No one could have predicted it. Not even Joey.

The Mighty Plumbers won the opening tip-off. Skinny Dennis tipped the ball to Joey, who dribbled under the legs of a Nike defender and darted—quick as a flea—to our end of the court.

Joey got downcourt so fast that no one else was within twenty feet. So he took his time dribbling underneath the basket, stopped, took a big breath, and heaved the ball up and into the hoop.

The entire Spiro home crowd went crazy. (Except for Mother T, who sat silently with hands folded over her lap.)

Then Becky pulled off a shifty move. After the basket, a Nike player prepared to inbound the ball to a teammate. Becky faked as if she wasn't looking, but at the last second she stepped in front of the pass, grabbed the ball, and scored.

Carlos, Jimmy, and I jumped up off the bench. We each pumped a fist into the air and, with the other hand, waved one of Ricky's clean and fragrant towels overhead.

The Spiro cheerleaders bounced up and down and shook their teal-colored pom-pom thingies. The Spiro T. Agnew dumpy gym's high-tech "light show" went off.

Derp!

Nevertheless, in the first few seconds of the game, Spiro had grabbed the Big Mo.

Our players had locked in on Coach Earwax's game plan.

On offense, Joey was the "quarterback"

of the team. He passed off to Becky, Dewey, Stephanie, and Skinny whenever they were open.

And on defense? The Mighty Plumbers were lean, mean, and focused.

We played quick, but we didn't hurry.

At halftime, the Mighty Plumbers were creaming the Platypuses, 50–22.

CHAPTER 28

The second half of the game was a complete reversal of game momentum.

What happened at halftime inside the visiting team's squalid locker room?

Maybe the Nike Prep coach screamed at his players and told them they were weak and useless and were getting slaughtered by the Mighty Plumbers inside our dump of a gymnasium.

Or maybe the Platypuses coach just told

them to never give up.

"Think positive!"

Whatever it was, the Big Mo shifted.

The Nike Prep point guard, charged right at Joey. He used his height advantage to spot teammates who broke toward the basket. Then he passed the ball and they scored.

The Platypuses poured it on.

Joey kept penetrating the Nike Prep defenses, but they had adjusted to his flea-like speed and cut him off. Then they either blocked our shots or grabbed rebounds if we missed.

And on the other end of the court, the Platypuses passed the ball, looked for the open player, and scored easy baskets. It was a total unselfish team effort.

The Mighty Plumbers were getting outscored and outhustled and outrebounded.

Nike Prep had the Big Mo and built a 60–50 lead with only a minute to go. The Platypuses fans were on their feet and chanting as if they had the Big Game totally in the bag.

The Spiro side of the gym was silent.

Coach Earwax called a time-out and gathered us on the sideline. He took a knee and scribbled a few mysterious lines on his whiteboard, but then he chucked it aside and stood up.

Coach pointed at me. I thought he meant that I should get ready to do the Rally Slide.

But I was wrong.

I replaced Dewey in the lineup. Coach needed a lean, mean rebounding machine. But the Mighty Plumbers needed the Big Mo now more than ever. If I was in the game, who would do the Rally Slide?

Coach pointed at Jimmy.

"Do that belly slide thingy."

On my way onto the court, I looked back. Jimmy was stretching out in front of the bench in preparation for the Rally Slide.

Then I noticed something moving underneath the bench. At first I thought it was that gym rat nosing around in search of tasty protein bars. But it wasn't the rat.

It was Fido!

My snake had stowed away in my sports bag, and now he was crawling out onto the floor only a few inches away from Jimmy's feet.

And I happen to know from an incident in baseball season that Jimmy suffers from ophidiophobia—a morbid fear of snakes!

I thought about running back to the bench and stashing Fido back in my bag before he scared Jimmy right out of his skull and ruined the Rally Slide, but it was too late.

The referee blew his whistle to resume the game.

CHAPTER

29

Jimmy Jimerino—Spiro's hotshot BJOC—pulled off an excellent Rally Slide. He slid ten feet on his belly like a baseball player diving to snag a line drive. The Spiro fans immediately jumped to their feet and cheered.

In the final minute of the game, the Mighty Plumbers played quick but we didn't hurry.

Joey controlled the ball and dished passes to Becky, Stephanie, and Skinny. I went to work on the boards. In my mind, I pictured my backyard hoop next to Mr. Verheyen's super-chill chickens. I started hauling down rebounds, one after another.

We had the Big Mo, and the Nike Prep lead began to shrink.

I was able to take a quick glance at the bench. Fido was nowhere to be seen. Jimmy had been spared, but I had no idea where my pet had gone.

With less than ten seconds remaining in the game, Nike Prep was ahead, 71–70. We had enough time for one last shot.

Joey took the inbounds pass and dashed down the floor. At the top of the key, he stopped and quickly looked around. I was the only one open.

Joey passed me the ball. The clock was down to three seconds.

I was going to take the shot, but at the last instant, I spotted Joey. He and I made eye contact, and I think he read my mind.

In that split second, I remembered Joey's

amazing flea-like leap when he knocked the basketball that was stuck on the top of the hoop.

So instead of a bounce pass to Joey, I lobbed an alley-oop pass high above the rim. Joey leaped like a flea, caught the ball in midair, and then landed on the rim!

Joey didn't dunk. He simply *dropped* the basketball into the hoop.

And I'm not even making that up!

The Mighty Plumbers defeated the Platy-puses, 72–71. We were the league champions for the first time in the history of Spiro T. Agnew Middle School.

Our fans flowed out of the bleachers and onto the court. Joey jumped down off the hoop and was immediately mobbed by me and the other players. Jimmy Jimerino picked him up and placed him on his shoulders.

Joey and I exchanged high fives and fist bumps.

"Nice dunk!"

"Nice pass!"

During the celebration, Coach Earwax complimented Jimmy on his excellent Rally Slide.

I traded hugs with Stephanie and Becky, then broke off and went to search for Fido. I was worried that he might have wandered onto the court, where he would get squashed by the celebrating fans.

But Fido was safe. He'd slithered out from under the bleachers and crawled over to me. He was unharmed, but there was a big bulge in his belly. And it was about the size of a gym rat.

EPILOGUE

So I wasn't exactly the hotshot athlete hero of the Big Game, but my hard work in the backyard paid off, and I got to be a lean, mean rebounding machine in the final minutes of the Big Game.

Anyway, I don't even want to be a hotshot athlete hero. I'm okay with sitting on the pine.

I'm probably better at it than anyone else my age in the entire universe. End of the bench. Middle of the bench. Doesn't matter.

No brag. It's just a fact.

ABOUT THE AUTHOR

STEVE MOORE is a rookie author, amateur cartoonist, and C+ student at Spiro T. Agnew Middle School.

When his rear end isn't glued to the bench along with his two best friends, Joey Linguini and Carlos Diaz, Steve likes to spend time selling sports memorabilia at inflated prices and hanging out with his pets—especially Fido, a large snake who struggles with separation anxiety.

Steve does not like to spend time eating broccoli, running wind sprints until his lungs explode, or climbing into the attic to dispose of dead rats.

He lives with his former hotshot athlete dad and turbo-hyper-worrywart mom in the extraordinarily average city of Goodfellow, which may or may not show up on Google Maps.

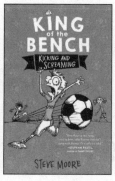
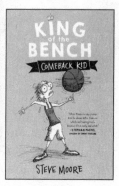